Mani Obhrai was born and lives in London, which is somewhere in the United Kingdom. He enjoys tea, chips, beer, cricket, Morris dancing, bulldogs and double-decker buses. He is regularly spotted wearing a pin-striped suit, carrying a newspaper under his arm, shouting, "Cheerio!"

False Memory

15 stories that I think are actually true

First published 2007

This paperback edition published 2007

A CIP catalogue record for this book is available from the British Library

ISBN 978-1-84799-022-8

1

This book is dedicated to those who have strived to make my life easier. For the most part, these people probably know who they are, but in case there is any doubt, they are listed below. If you did not make my life easier in any way, but would still like, for some reason, to have this book dedicated to you, please write your name in the space provided below and feel free to show it to your friends and loved ones, or simply to people you might wish to impress.

Thanks to: Paige Baird, _______________, Serena Obhrai, Greer Baird, Indy Lalli and Amy Laurence for all their help with editing and moral support.

Introduction by the author

"So, I'm going to write a book."

"Oh, really? What's it going to be about?"

"Well, I'm not entirely sure. I'll write about things that have happened to me and things that I've seen. It should be interesting."

"What? Who'd want to read that? I mean, who wants to read a bunch of true stories? True stories are usually pretty boring."

"You don't understand – I've experienced some strange things!"

"Sure, I know. But are they interesting and exciting enough that people will want to read about them?"

"I think so. I hope so."

"You know what I think? I think you should fictionalise them. Add extra stuff in. Make them funny, exciting, whatever. "

"I don't need to do that… Do I?"

"I know you better than you know yourself. You should do it."

"I'm going to write what really happened. The stories will be fine… I think."

"Come on, let's do it together. Alright? It'll be great."

"Uh… Alright."

"Good. Let's begin"

"Wait a minute. How can we do it together? This is my book."

"Sure it is…"

The triangular white stain

I was on the London Underground[1] on the way to work, as I often am, when I was wrenched from my lonely boredom, at Euston[2] if I remember correctly, by a rather large man forcing his way onto the carriage with a multitude of luggage items the weight of which could probably crush to death most members of the healthy male species.

What first struck me about this man was not the fact that he was rather large, but that he had a triangular white stain on his face, just below and to the side of his lower lip, which was itself also rather large. For the triangle connoisseurs among you and those with obsessive-compulsive disorder, it was pointing directly up towards the sky, or where I believe the sky would have been[3] had I been able to see it.

My curiosity sufficiently aroused, and believing this to be a first-rate opportunity to reduce the mundanity of my trip, I shuffled around in the meagre space afforded me, avoiding the elderly passengers of which there seemed to be an excessive amount for the time of day, trying to remain inconspicuous but conscious that time was running out, in order to get a better vantage point.

After the large man had successfully boarded the train with his aforementioned baggage, he was able to take a short breather, and while the carriage doors slowly closed, sealing him safely inside, his hand started inching in a tantalising manner towards his face.

That was when I saw it.

The cause of the triangular white stain, and probably a few more of the large man's problems[4], was a fresh cream cake, about the size of a 3-month-old baby's head.

The triangular white stain melted into a kite, then a steamboat, then a butterfly moth, and then nothingness…

The great pencil heist of '85

The hot sun bore down on the other children in the playground, as I sat on the step, as bored as ever, after having just ended my poor attempt to eat the carbohydrate-filled meal that was served to me as an excuse for lunch.

Out of the corner of my eye, I saw Goebbels, a short stocky boy from my class with an angry face and a gait that looked as though it had been stolen from an elderly tightrope walker with Parkinson's. I pondered this as he met my gaze, discreetly acknowledged my nod, and meandered over, arms held out at his sides.

Talking to Goebbels was like trying to explain the fundamentals of string theory to a toddler, and after what seemed like a few hours had passed, he had a attained a basic understanding of my plan. Its premise was simple: steal every writing implement from our classroom and get out without being seen.

The obvious potential ramifications of recruiting Goebbels immediately began playing on my potato-addled mind, but I was young and liked to give the impression that I enjoyed life on the edge, if only to enhance my fledgling social status.

Time, in those days, was at a premium[5], so we left at once for our classroom on the first floor. Astounding though it may seem, we encountered nobody on the journey up and were in intoxicatingly high spirits upon reaching our destination.

We instantly set to work, searching the room for pens and pencils, our inexperience manifesting itself outwardly as nonchalance as we neglected to even close the door. The hunt was over quickly, resulting in a pile of pencils on one of the desks, which for some reason made me recall the fact that I had never been fishing[6].

At this point, however, our tale begins its decline into tragedy; with a slightly bewildered look on my face, as though being controlled by some devilish force, I took as much of the pile as I could carry and put it down closer to the window. Glancing down at the children, blissfully unaware of their fate, I chuckled quietly to myself. Goebbels silently followed me with the remainder of the pile and watched with indifference as I lobbed a pencil out of the window.

A few seconds passed before I looked at Goebbels to find that he was holding up a pencil and looking at me sheepishly, and so I nodded, comprehensively but in a serious manner.

His pencil flew in an arc out into the sunshine and then we became demons, possessed, throwing the pencils out into the big wide world.

As we embarked on our journey back to the playground, I beamed proudly while reflecting that not one of the children outside had noticed our lead-filled projectiles.

The remainder of the lunch hour passed without incident and I returned to the classroom having, in fact, completely forgotten about my plot, and was only reminded when seeing the dribbling grin on Goebbels' face. Within a few minutes, the teacher had received 24 complaints from pupils about missing pencils. To keep up the ruse, even I complained; it could even be argued I was one of the most outspoken complainants.

The interrogation session was long and hard. The teacher threatened us with detentions, extra homework, and even letters home, but nobody said a word. After many hours[7] of this, to no avail, she began to give up, when, Goebbels slowly and gingerly raised his hand, his face showing signs of reminiscence combined with extreme ecstasy, and I genuinely believe he did not realise what he was about to do.

Of course, looking back, I ended up the worst off. But I learned something that I have kept with me to this day and impart to anyone who cares to listen: choose your sidekick wisely.

Willie's accident

Willie's celebratory meal was held at a tiny Greek restaurant[8] in Primrose Hill, and on that fateful evening the ouzo was flowing freely. Willie was, just as he preferred, the centre of attention: Australian, tall with broad shoulders, stuffed into what looked suspiciously like Captain Birdseye's white sailing uniform and hat.

He was on good form during the reasonably priced meal, and I reflected that Willie could probably have made a decent career as an above average stand-up comedian had he put his overtly twisted but competently funny mind to it. I noticed by the comments they made, that his friends, some of whom were here on holiday, were thinking similar thoughts as they tucked into their fried calamari and Lamb Fricassee.

As the alarmingly stereotypical Greek waiter collected the bill, Willie asked if anyone would like to continue celebrating his first stab at country and western disc jockeying, at the conveniently situated nearby flat that he had somehow arranged to rent for a pittance, and it was testament to Willie, despite it being a Sunday, that everyone present, including the waiter, agreed that this was a good idea.

Within a short time, which seemed like a few minutes but could have been anything up to an hour, we were at Willie's flat, and I decided to relieve him of his music-playing duties. Seeing as his collection was almost entirely composed of them, I chose to play something from one of the many *Triple J Hottest 100*[9] CDs he had amassed, presumably before he moved to London. The night continued joyfully and within the confines of safety until about 4am.

That was about the time when Gerry Rafferty's *Baker Street* reverberated through the speakers.

At this point Willie requested my accompaniment for a dance, probably eager to display some newly acquired saxophone-related moves to his infrequently seen acquaintances.

Several seconds, four misplaced feet and the legs of the coffee table duly conspired to cause me to hurtle backwards, with Willie tumbling forwards towards me. Time itself toyed with us to allow us both to deeply ponder how drunk we really could have been to possibly end up in this unfavourable predicament, heading for almost certain trouble. The glass coffee table stayed defiantly intact as my back exploded against it, however the crystal wine glass that Willie's face collided with was shattered, helped along by our planet's often-lamented force of gravity.

Willie's internal gyroscope activated itself in conjunction with his concern circuits and he immediately stood upright, effortlessly lifting me with him, asking if I was hurt. I was too shocked to respond, mesmerised by the blood spraying from the 3-inch long, exquisitely straight slit in his left temple through which I was certain that bone could be spied; this reminded me of countless movies where I had witnessed similar scenes and wrongly dismissed them as being unrealistic.

No one can say with confidence where things would have ended up had there not been a physician on-site, and it was indeed her who calmly took the situation under control.

She expertly stemmed the scarlet tide while a taxi was hastily called to take us to the nearest hospital. Time seemed to slow as we waited, but Willie himself seemed strangely to be coping very well under the extremely adverse conditions he was being subjected to, and, in fact, could only mumble about the scar he envisioned himself gaining, and the wonders it would do for his chances with women.

Five hours, sixteen stitches and a bedtime story later, Willie was back at his flat, safely tucked up in bed murmuring in a semi-lucid state about his future scar, and I was finally able to think about heading for home. It was a bizarre experience travelling home on the underground during the Monday morning rush hour, watching the suits through my bleary sleep-deprived eyes. I realised I must have been exuding an unsavoury odour as a by-product of the evening's adventures, as wherever I went, *Metro*[10] newspaper in hand, my fellow commuters cleared a wide path for me.

Upon arriving home, absolutely shattered and in need of some well-earned sleep, I realised that in all the excitement, I had forgotten to visit the toilet, and was by now fairly desperate, so decided to use the lavatory before continuing. After an extensive leak, the colour and texture of which I shan't dwell upon, I washed my hands, the stains on which I couldn't begin to determine the source of, and looked in the mirror, only to discover the reason behind my 5-star treatment on the London Underground.

Because it was only then that I noticed Willie's blood, thickly caked down one side of my face.

Rental van

It was an exceptionally bright and sunny day in June and we were heading to Glastonbury[11] for the big and fairly regular annual music festival. But first we had to pick up the van; Willie and I both agreed that a camper van would be safer and more comfortable than sleeping in tents and exposing our lives and belongings to the risks of danger and theft respectively.

We arrived at the rental yard in Notting Hill[12] in the early afternoon, but as we approached, it was clear that something was awry.

The haggard rental man bore the heavy weight of defeat as he surrendered the bad news: there was a problem with the van and it wasn't safe to drive.

The surface of the planet fell away at my feet and I descended into the uncharted depths of the Earth, jagged rock walls closing in on all sides, everything slowly receding into blackness.

I jolted from my nightmare to see the van up on blocks, mechanics scurrying around it like demented rats around a giant block of Monterey Jack, the rental man detailing the multitude of faults with it. But I couldn't hear a word. The dark reality hit me with the stark surprise of a pedestrian hit in the back by a cyclist jumping a red light: there was no way we would find another van in time; we were going to have to sleep in tents.

Perhaps I should stop here to explain my dislike for tents. On second thoughts, maybe simply listing the harsh disadvantages of camping is enough: mud, insects, angered animals, thieves, adverse weather effects and, of course, the little known but very real risk of prostate cancer[13].

A few seconds later, and we had finally given up, and were about to leave, when the rental man told us of one of his acquaintances: a man named Big

Ned who ran a car lot nearby. Big Ned apparently had a camper van and might be persuaded to rent it to us.

Big Ned's car lot was an intimidating place; burly, hairy men patrolled, most likely keeping an eye out for anyone who may have noticed any of the clearly stolen vehicles dotted around the massive area. There was no sign of Big Ned, though we were told he would be back soon from an 'errand'.

Big Ned finally arrived, and if the emphatically butch patrolmen were scary, he himself was the epitome of fear inspiring; his name positively understated how large he actually was. With the gift of hindsight I truly believe his mother would have christened him Gargantuan Ned.

Cowering slightly from the giant, who wore little but a string vest, our voices increased an octave as we introduced ourselves and gently enquired about his camper van.

His laugh boomed as he folded his arms, completing a surreal caricature of himself, and then explained that the van was his 5.1 litre pride and joy, and that he wouldn't let it out of his sight.

I pictured myself with Willie, sharing a sleeping bag in a half-standing tent, raindrops leaking through huge holes that conveniently allowed us to keep an eye on the possessions that had been unworthy even for thieves, strewn on the grass outside.

As the pitch of my voice incremented another notch, I asked nicely if he would rent us his lovely left-hand drive Dodge Ram if we promised to really, really look after it.

To my utter surprise, he agreed, adding however that if we damaged it, he would damage us, and that of course I'd need to be temporarily added to his insurance policy.

After entering his tiny office hut, handing him my driver's licence and watching him put it into his drawer, then tap some keys on what looked suspiciously like a BBC Micro[14] that wasn't even switched on, he said we were all set and he could get the van ready for us. Not wanting to cause any further delay, I smiled, feigning ignorance.

Outside, he hailed some of his minions to empty the van, while an extremely old lady miraculously appeared from the seemingly empty office. To this day that is probably the most visually impressive live magic trick I have the pleasure of witnessing. The old lady and I watched the contents of the van slowly emptied onto the ground, while Willie was being taught by Big Ned about how to look after the van - where to pour the water, what it liked to have for breakfast, and so forth.

As the final item was removed from the van - an industrial compressed gas cylinder along with 100 feet of piping - I marvelled at the pile of stuff that had been created - it looked enough to fill 3 or 4 average-size transit vans.

Big Ned said his farewells to his van, and then we were ready. He stifled back tears as he waved, watching as Willie navigated the van down the narrow side street.

Waving back via the wing mirror, I'm sure I saw Big Ned flinch as we clipped the left kerb, then the right, heading for another adventure…

Carly

It was just another night at the Marathon Kebab in Chalk Farm, a place known far and wide for its delicious burgers[15] and intermittent lecherous activity. To the untrained eye it looked like a kebab shop imbued with history, tradition, culture and steadfast efficiency, but setting foot in the back room was akin to entering an exciting and brave new world. Back there was a bar and live music, courtesy of the rockabilly performer who is still sometimes seen busking on the Northern Line of the London Underground, using his erratic charisma and raw musical talent to gather what funds he can in order to buy himself just a little more crack.

In most respects, this was not an unusual evening: I was there with a couple of friends, and the place was packed with other misfits and social outcasts; this was not the place to go for decadent company and relaxed but slightly competitive conversation about newly purchased power drills, but those wanting to get completely wasted and have some ambiguous fun would probably find something beyond what they were looking for.

As usual it was too busy to find anywhere to sit down, so we stood there with our drinks, shouting our respective sides of the conversation over the finely tuned music and spasmodic grunts and barks.

That was when she tapped me on the shoulder.

I turned to face her and she asked me in her thick Scottish accent if I would do her a favour, her spittle spraying wildly; her friend had gone to use the facilities and she wondered if I might sit on the empty stool to stop it being taken in the meantime by one of the many socially inept down-and-outs staggering about. Alcohol tends to enhance my general level of politeness, so I assented, somewhat reluctantly, sitting down and introducing myself.

Her name was Carly. A name I felt no adverse reaction to, but would soon grow to fear even more than spending three and a half years of my life in a coma after a high speed motorcycle accident, one of my groundless phobias. We engaged in some small talk; she swigged from her can of Tennent's Super[16] and I mused about how old she was. The lack of available light hindered the decision-making process, but I finally settled for the 50 to 60 age bracket, mentally raising a triumphant fist to the air.

She lit a cigarette from her pack of Camels and took an unnecessarily long drag, visibly trying to gauge my thoughts. Both of my friends looked on in amusement, one of them even giving me an unwelcome thumbs-up, as Carly began to barrage me with chat-up lines that would not have looked out of place in the pages of a self-help book, her sweaty jowl flapping with excitement. She asked me if I went there often, whether I was having a good time, and what I would be doing after leaving at 2am when the place would invariably be raided by police; she added that she lived very close by; she even threw in as a bizarre afterthought that back at her place, she 'had music'.

I pride myself on being a paragon of good manners, and in situations like this it can be difficult to escape untainted; I did my best to subtly spurn her advances without upsetting her, however this did have the wholly unintentional and undesired side effect of leaving her feeling as though she was still in with a statistical chance of success. When, after sitting with her for the best part of an hour, I asked where her friend was, she smiled sheepishly, showing jagged, yellow-brown teeth, and told me she made it all up in order to break the ice. More flattery. I found it impossible to relieve myself of the stool, and cursed my good manners for letting me down like this.

2am arrived and, like clockwork, so did the nightly police raid. Fearing for my safety, Carly pleaded with me not to get involved, probably not realising that that would be the last thing I'd want to do. Everyone was slowly ushered from the establishment, where a row of cabs waited for business. My friends were from out of London and had arranged to stay with me, but for some reason I felt a tinge of guilt about leaving Carly behind, and hence foolishly resolved to personally make sure that she got home safe.

So when I told the driver our destination, I added that we'd need to drop one of our number off just around the corner. Carly heard this and looked at me like a retarded child who had opened her solitary birthday present expecting a BMX bicycle but actually finding a pair of socks for school. The four of us got into the taxi, Carly straining what remained of her guile and technique to procure a seat in the back beside me.

From here on, her tactics, as well as her level of desperation, went into overdrive; she told me she was lonely, begged me to go home with her, and, painfully, sang into my ear, along to *You're so Vain* by her namesake Carly Simon, which in a cruel twist of fate was playing on the radio.

By the time we pulled up outside her flat, Carly's cunning had almost depleted, but she had already conceived the final part of her plan. The car stopped, and she opened the door and stepped out, patting herself down fairly suggestively and loudly wondering where her keys were. She stood there for some time feeling sorry for herself, still pretending to search for her keys.

There was only one thing I could do. I slammed the door shut, looked at the driver and shouted one word:

"Drive!"

Afflicted

I dropped a tea bag into my favourite mug and poured in some water from the kettle. It was winter break - I had some time off from university and my aim was to do as little as possible, even though, according to the hugely elaborate, arctic wildlife themed revision timetable in my free hand, I was meant to be studying Numerical Analysis, one of the many subjects I would probably fail definitively upon my return. Waiting for the tea to brew, I stirred in some sugar whilst fascinatedly reading about the considerably varying gestation period of polar bears.

If there were a scale to measure unexpectedness, what happened next would have been, in my eyes, grounds for the international organisation responsible for this scale to review their standards.

I clutched my chest as the pain tore through me, and as I fell to the floor I took a moment to wonder whether this was what a heart attack felt like; it certainly seemed plausible. After a few minutes of constant writhing and indignant groans of distress, most of which I added intentionally in order to enhance the effect, I managed to amass the energy and fortitude to lift myself up. The left side of my upper torso was still in intense agony, but I was confident that I had attained sufficient tolerance to cope with it for the time being.

I took some painkillers, which eventually returned my power of thought, and I tried to self-diagnose my affliction; in the end I settled for 'nasty, disagreeable heartburn' and did my utmost to continue my day as I had been accustomed: procrastinating, as well as popping paracetamol and ibuprofen considerably more often than the safe intervals declared on their packets.

A day or two passed, and the pain had not yet departed, forcing my extreme stubbornness to belatedly relent; I then gained the freedom to decide that it would make sense to see a doctor.

The examination was over quickly; the doctor said he couldn't immediately see anything wrong but, as a precaution, sent me to the minor accident centre[17] a short walk away for an X-ray.

It was almost the end of a quiet working day, and it wasn't long before I was strapped into a futuristic machine and provided with my recommended daily allowance of X-rays, and between the beeps and whirrs I couldn't help but wonder whether the story of the Incredible Hulk had any foundation in science[18].

Alone in the waiting room afterwards, I flicked through some magazines. I couldn't concentrate, not even on the photos of brand new hi-fi equipment and infidelity amongst Z-list celebrities. My mind was rattling with questions: was I morbidly ill? Would I die young? Would I ever make any real friends? Did the 1969 moon landing really happen?

While sitting there, I realised that if I sat in the northernmost seat and leaned 45 degrees to my left, I could clearly hear the two staff members in the next room. They were examining my X-ray. I looked around the empty room, wondering what would be said next.

"What's that? A cyst?"

Dark thoughts began to stagger and claw their way through my already congested mind. The walls in the waiting room started to slowly close in. The light dimmed and flickered. The whole room spun and shook.

"That's not a cyst – it's a tumour."

If my heart was racing earlier, now it was standing on the winner's podium, spraying onlookers with champagne. I started to feel dizzy and, all logic having seemingly evaporated from my normally cloudless brain, I stood and swayed towards the source of the voices, the light growing so dim now that I could barely see. The grim reaper himself suddenly appeared, wielding a scythe and blocking the doorway, his red eyes the only things visible beneath his black hood. He stood there, somehow mocking me without moving or making a sound.

Then he started to emit a low hum and began to slowly transform; his dark cloak shifted through increasingly lighter shades, via infinite greys, until it was white; his face gradually became visible; his scythe morphed into a drip feed trolley. Before I knew what was going on, there was a doctor standing before me, who told me I would need to be taken to a hospital for treatment. He wouldn't elaborate, despite my pleading; instead I was asked to lie on a bed and allow nurses to attach monitoring equipment to me, an act I would, under normal circumstances, have most likely have taken some enjoyment from.

Not wanting to be the centre of attention on such an unfortunate day, I told them I was happy to get a bus to the hospital, but they insisted that I wait for the ambulance to arrive.

The paramedics duly arrived, preceded by their high-pitched wail and flashing blue lights, and carried me on a stretcher into the back of their van, while I repeatedly proclaimed my new mantra: I was happy to make my own way, I was happy to make my own way, I was happy to make my own way. However, I was completely ignored, and instead an oxygen mask was strapped to my face, to "shut the annoying boy up", as one of the attendants put it. The siren was utilised once or twice to get through some rough spots and, all in all, we reached the hospital in good time.

There I was left on a bed before the paramedics zoomed off to halt another emergency. I had time to ponder my situation and wondered why I had not been divulged the extent of my injury. Fearing the worst, I sat back and tried to think about the good times I had experienced during my short life: Sundays in the park having ice cream with Rover the dog[19]; inventing groundbreaking new products only to have them stolen by multinational conglomerates; teaching cats to love and respect stuffed toy fish.

I dazed in and out of a dream state until a young doctor approached me. He cheerfully explained to me that I had a partially collapsed lung, referred to amongst his colleagues at dinner parties as a pneumothorax[20]. Part of the lung had caved in, released some air into my thorax and this was causing the pain. I was told I had options as to my treatment: they could either force a rubber tube into my throat to suck the trapped air out, or I could take some special tablets for the pain, and over time the air would slowly disperse. I had to decide...

Seven days later and I was at home, mulling over the events of the week. The last of the air had finally escaped my body, relieving me of my suffering. I sat back, grinning widely at the straight A grades I had achieved in my exam results.

It's amazing what a doctor's note will do for you.

ICE NO ICE

Darkness surrounded me; the only light originated from the perpetually humming contraption. At that moment it was as though nothing else existed. I glanced at the small sign in front of me and fought impulse. I wanted to push the button, but something inside told me not to. Somewhere, the second-hand of a clock was slowly moving, its ticking echoing around the inside of my skull.

I squinted in an attempt to block out some of the white light coming from the machine. In front of me was a button, with a small sign next to it. I'd lost count how many times I had already mused over its meaning. I read it again.

ICE NO ICE

Its cryptic nature taunted me; I was lost as to its significance. I needed to push the button. I needed to find out.

I pondered over past experiences and decided that there were only two types of regret: regret over things that had been done, and regret over things that hadn't. I always felt the latter was worse. Hindsight is a wonderful thing, but a missed opportunity can be remembered for a long time.

The logical part of my brain told me I didn't want to press the button, but my heart and soul were both intent on it. Could it cause more trouble than it was worth? Probably. I reasoned that the button couldn't possibly do anything useful, could it? Therefore, by deduction, the situation could only stay the same or get worse. Perhaps I was thinking about it too much. But I still felt compelled to push it. I had to... Didn't I? Curiosity is a worrying, but natural part of the human condition.

I was befuddled; I couldn't think straight. The humming was intensifying and the light was getting brighter. I felt as though I had been there for hours; my eyelids were getting heavier and heavier. My body was slowly giving in – I needed sleep. But I also needed to know what the button was for.

A cold draught hit me and I shivered. The hairs on the back of my neck were wide-awake, but the rest of my body felt as though it would collapse at any moment. If I were going to press the button, I would need to do it soon.

So I did it: I pushed the button. Firmly. Unequivocally. Irreversibly.

That was when everything went black.

I opened my eyes to find myself in a familiar bed, daylight and birdsong streaming in through the windows. Somewhere, children could be heard playing. I got up and padded into the kitchen.

There was a huge pool of water on the floor and I realised immediately what I had done. I opened the refrigerator door as my jaw dropped in horror.

I looked again at the sign, poorly translated from Japanese, and sighed.

ICE NO ICE

I had defrosted the icebox.

Bursting

"Wake up... Can you hear me? Wake up."

I opened my eyes. The room was so bright that I instinctively closed them again. The nurse asked me how I felt, and I responded by nonchalantly asking for her telephone number; I was euphoric, untouchable. Morphine will do that to you.

Though I spent the next few minutes inviting the nurses out on dates, my head flopping around on my neck like I was an old rag doll, they were doing a sterling job of putting up with me.

What was I doing there? Oh, yes: I had been diagnosed with appendicitis and it was decided that I needed to go under the knife. I had enquired as to whether my tonsils, which to me were just a set of useless throat ephemera, could also be taken out while I was there, but the surgeon just laughed and told me that they actually helped stop throat infections. Maybe you do learn something every day.

An orderly pushed my bed, drip-feed and all, to the ward where I was to spend the next three days, asking me politely to keep the noise down; apparently it had gone midnight and most of the other patients were asleep. I agreed, but only after being sated by some childish snickering and an impromptu sing-along.

The ward was sedate, and although I was so cheerful that I wanted to leap from the bed like Gene Kelly and recreate the famous dance scene from *Singin' in the Rain*, I did my best to try to keep quiet. It was dark, but I could see that there were two rows of beds, and that every occupant seemed to be in slumber. The orderly asked me to get some rest before he scurried off.

I'm not sure whether it was the effect of the drugs, the fact that I had to have a thermometer inserted into my ear every hour, the elderly patient who had a sneezing and laughing fit at two minute intervals, or simply that my bed was in a half-upright position, but I couldn't sleep.

At some point during the night, I opened my eyes, and was surprised to see the silhouette of a dishevelled man standing over me, snorting quietly, like I imagine a nervous pig would; it was so dark that I couldn't see his face. He scuttled towards me, raising his thin arms into the air, and when he reached the bed he began howling, wolf-like. Needless to say, I was fairly alarmed by his behaviour, but my vocal chords failed me. I wanted very much to cry for help, but instead I was frozen and just stared bemusedly and inquisitively, much like a baby might gape at the first piece of solid waste it ever saw leave its body.

Thankfully, the nurses noticed the shrieking, and came to take the strange man away. To this day, I am not sure who this man was, or even whether the entire spectacle was just a drug-fuelled fantasy.

Morning arrived, and the morphine had worn off. I felt fine, apart from the pain caused by my brand new three-inch incision. The surgeon had come to tell me the exciting good news: my appendix had been removed successfully and after close examination it had been determined that it was 'most definitely infected'. All I could do was wonder to myself what he would have told me if it hadn't been problematic and had been extracted without good reason.

The early part of the day was no extravaganza, and I soon needed to empty my abounding bowels. I called a nurse over; she said I was unfit to leave my bed and brought me a bedpan before pulling the curtains around me for privacy. She then asked me if I needed any help. After toying with the idea for a few seconds, I declined, trying to remember whether she was one of the nurses I had asked out the night before; I was in a different frame of mind then. I resolved to find out later.

She left me alone and I edged into position holding the bedpan; this took a while owing to my general discomfort and immobility, but I finally got myself situated. Then I waited.

Nothing happened.

I waited some more. Nothing.

I called the nurse and explained my predicament, but she told me it was normal after an operation to have these sensations, and that when my body was ready to 'go', it would.

Over the next hour, I tried again three times. My desperation increased with each attempt, until I decided that I was in official disagreement with the nurse; in my opinion, and for whatever reason, I just couldn't bring myself to do it. So I hatched a plan.

I carefully got out of bed, being sure to do this on the side with my drip-feed trolley, and hobbled towards the curtain, dragging my trolley along after me. I glanced out; I didn't want the nurse seeing what I was about to do.

The coast was clear.

I shuffled out into the open, pulling the trolley after me, its wheels squealing like a mouse facing certain death. I scrutinised the ward, scanning for my goal: a sign for the toilets. I soon spied something that may have fit this description in the adjoining corridor but I couldn't be sure: I could only see part of it. I moved towards it with the speed and agility of a long-term sufferer of motor neurone disease, all the while keeping an eye out for the nurse with the bad advice.

Reaching the corridor, I almost cried in delight: the sign was indeed for the toilets. I inched my way in the direction it recommended, and eventually I reached the entrance; I was almost there.

Upon arrival, I heaved myself into a cubicle, and began the eradication of my unwanted heftiness.

Afterwards, I felt like a new man.

I made the return journey with a similar level of vigilance and attention, avoiding any patrolling staff with what I believed to be the stealth of a ninja encumbered by a Zimmer frame. I had made it about half way back when I had the uneasy feeling I was being watched. It took me about a minute to turn around in the state I was in, but when I did, I saw him.

At the time I could not be completely certain of my suspicion, and even now, when I look back, I still have my doubts, but for a split-second he reminded me of the unkempt man who had startled me the night before. Was it his haggard appearance? His stick-like arms? The look of pure and utter hatred in his eyes? I couldn't be sure, but I was more than eager to get back to the realm of safety promised by my uncomfortable bed. I took another minute to turn back around, and then continued my limped voyage, fearing I would at any moment be feeling his breath on my neck, or worse.

I willed my legs to move faster, and slowly but surely they did; the old agility was seeping back into my crippled frame. I moved as fast as I could but the footsteps behind me were getting closer. It was a physical impossibility – I could not travel quickly enough to escape.

My curtain-enclosed bed was in sight. I was almost there when a firm finger suddenly prodded me on the shoulder. Hesitantly, I turned my head to face my pursuer, fearing the worst.

A huge sigh of relief left my lungs. It was my favourite nurse, and I was so incredibly glad it was she, that an unfaltering smile attached itself to my face. She gave me a severe telling off and helped me back into my bed, while I grinned maniacally at her.

"Anyway", she added, "you didn't need to do that."

She pointed to a door that was less than a foot from the head of my bed. The smile fell from my face and I held my head in my hands. The door had a tiny sign on it: 'Toilet.'

Plastic and clicks

The pebble skidded across the tarmac as it left my unfashionable boot and hurtled across the road. I was walking home from school, contemplating my forthcoming holiday; in a few weeks I would be going to Paris with some relatives and I wasn't looking forward to the time away from my classmates.

As I stepped through the front door and removed my jacket, the phone rang. I waited three rings, a compulsive habit of mine, and then answered. It was Arty, my best friend.

"What's plastic and clicks?" he asked mysteriously.

Bewildered, I shrugged pointlessly and told him that I didn't know. He hung up.

It took a few seconds, but I soon deduced the answer to his question: a telephone; it's plastic and it clicks when you hang up. Hilarious. Witty, even. I was used to antics like this from Arty; it was one of the reasons we were such good friends. I stored the new trick away safely into the *Pranks* area of my mental filing cabinet, wondering when in the future I would find a good opportunity to pull it out.

A few weeks later and I was sitting in a car at the Port of Dover. My aunt and uncle were in the front and I was in the back with their two sons, listening to the raindrops buffeting the bonnet. We were bored, having already driven for over two hours, and were now waiting to board the already late ferry to Calais. It looked like it would be a while longer, so I told everyone I was going to get some fresh air, and got out of the car.

There was a burger bar near the vehicle, and, not wanting to get too wet, I hurried inside. There wasn't much in there for those not wanting some poorly cooked ground beef in a bun, so I just stared at the patterns formed on the window by the rain. Among the things I spotted were an African elephant, an inverted abstraction of the Mona Lisa, and the number 9.

The mood in the restaurant was desolate, and this was only accentuated by the deplorable weather; everyone had a foul look on his or her face, even the children, all of them seemingly brought up without much in the way of etiquette. In the corner of the room, and afforded its own small private area, I noticed a public telephone.

An idea floated from the heavens, its wings two small parentheses; it bore through my skull, lacerated my cerebral cortex and came to a grinding halt in the epicentre of my frontal lobe[21].

Captivated, I sauntered to the telephone and lifted the handset. The dial tone serenaded my hypnotised ears. I punched in the number for the operator and waited. Within a few seconds a chirpy female voice greeted me. Startled into life, I rifled though my metaphysical filing system until I found what I was looking for.

"What's plastic and clicks?" I asked her.

I waited a second or so and then hung up; she didn't have time to respond. I chuckled to myself and decided to head back to the others.

Back in the car I chose to keep quiet about my caper in order to avoid any potential trouble with my aunt and uncle.

We waited some more; the ferry still wasn't ready.

We listened to the radio, played *I Spy* and ate crisps[22] whilst watching the seagulls being tossed about by the wind.

My ears pricked. Sirens could be heard in the distance.

Over the next few minutes, a convoy of fire engines appeared and the occupants jumped out, ready for action.

I froze. My jaw dropped. The vehicle suddenly felt half the size it had felt just a moment earlier. Dizziness took hold of me. If anyone in the car had been looking at me instead of the fire brigade, the consternation conveyed by my face would have given me away.

Was this something to do with the phone call I had made? When I thought about it, it was perfectly feasible that my question to the operator could have been misconstrued as a threat to trigger a timed plastic explosive.

Sitting in absolute silence, I watched; the firemen scuttled around, like worker ants, with looks of absolute concern on their faces. For about ten minutes, I scrutinised their frantic searching and anxious chatter, praying that nobody in the burger bar was smart enough to put two and two together. Slowly, the firemen became satisfied that they were dealing with a hoax.

Eventually, the nervousness amongst the firemen had been completely alleviated, and they began to get on their way.

After a further few moments they had all disappeared. I sighed in relief, and we returned to waiting patiently.

Finally the ferry was ready and the passengers gradually boarded, looking forward to their respective holidays.

Just over a week later, I was back in London. I had told Arty about the escapade, and we had both vowed never to unleash that particular shenanigan again. We had also arranged to call one another if either of us came up with an operator-safe gag.

I sat back on the sofa with a notepad and pen, mulling over my prior conversation with Arty, but I couldn't come up with any good ideas for telephone tomfoolery. As I sat there about to concede defeat, the phone rang. I dawdled for the obligatory three rings, and then picked it up.

"Hello there, this is an engineer from British Telecom. We are undertaking some maintenance on this line, so please don't use your phone for the next half an hour or so. If you do, there is a risk I will get an electric shock." the voice said, in a thick Somerset accent.

After assenting, I returned to the sofa and glanced through the pathetic scrawlings on my notepad. A few minutes later, the phone started to ring again, and I absent-mindedly answered it.

I shuddered in surprise as the engineer squealed, yelped and shrieked, the electric current passing through his jittering frame. The wailing continued for a few seconds before slowly devolving into manic, taunting laughter.

Arty was good.

Whisky

I observed the men at the table. They were drinking and joking and catching up – some of them hadn't seen one another in years. My father sat among them, tired and smiling; he had just flown into the country, and had brought with him some whisky especially for the occasion.

We were in a small village in New Delhi, India, in a cramped and unnecessarily cluttered room in an old house; I was trying to keep myself cool but failing miserably. The heat was stifling; I was covered in sweat, and my bottle of substandard cola wasn't helping me feel any better.

Although probably too young to truly appreciate alcoholic spirits, I had been bewitched by the whisky bottle all evening. I wasn't considered nearly old enough to be offered any, but that didn't stop me reading the label ad nauseam, until I had inadvertently memorised the information presented on it.

A little later in the evening, I got up and decided to go for a walk, but before I could reach the door, I was summoned to the table. A neat shot of Johnnie Walker Black Label was poured into a glass in front of me and I looked at it, unsure of how to approach this unfamiliar situation. I glanced again at the bottle as it sat there, contemptuously glaring at me with ridicule and intimidation: it was a 12-year-old blend, almost as old as I was, and it seemed to know it.

I made a concerted effort to breathe normally; everyone had their eyes on me – my ears felt as though they were turning red. Swallowing my fears, I took a careful sip and waited to see what effect it would have on me. It wasn't so bad – I didn't realise what all the fuss was about; I gulped the rest down in one. A couple of seconds later there was a searing pain in my throat, but I was in the company of grown men; I did my best not to flinch, though this had a cost: my eyes probably looked as though they were popping out of their sockets.

The table enthusiastically cheered my first ever whisky; its occupants emitted agreeable sounds and cheerfully nodded to each other. It seemed as though I had earned my way into the group. But I was curious: wasn't alcohol supposed to make you drunk? It didn't seem to be working; perhaps I was inexplicably immune.

The table got back to normality as the boisterousness resumed, and I was immediately supplied with another shot, which was swiftly dispatched with slightly less effort. I didn't experience anything out of the ordinary, and was of the impression that I could have continued all night.

But any knowledge of my level of consumption was soon mislaid; my head started to feel as though it weighed considerably less than it should have. Upon closing my eyes I was startled into opening them again by the unnerving perception of weightlessness. I became lost in erratic thought, imagining my eyes as two video cameras, capturing a real-time video feed and electronically transmitting this to the post-production unit that was my occipital lobe. But the feed had become incomprehensibly lagged: the impaired images I saw were a fraction of a second behind actual events.

In addition to the picture signal issues I was having, the alcohol had infiltrated my blood stream and was even in my ears, where it distorted the cupulas of my cochleas – this in turn offset my normally competent balance and caused the room to spin every time I moved my head even slightly.

The aural and visual complications made me feel uneasy; I needed to take a break, so I haphazardly slipped away from the swaying table and decided to go outside to get some air. Outside, I looked for some refuge in which to recover, as my condition worsened. It was a few minutes before I managed to regain a satisfactory level of control over my flailing motor functions. My confidence slowly returned, and I soon managed to look marginally less intoxicated than I actually was.

The moon shone down, lending its bleak light to the surroundings; though it was uncomfortably hot, it was a fairly gusty night and the periodic breeze helped clear my head. While I waited for nothing in particular, my back against a wall, a bothersome figure approached me.

It was one of the neighbours, a lanky teenager who was renowned for showing off and being a general irritation. He was walking alongside his bicycle, distractedly stroking its leather seat as he walked. He stopped as he neared, to give me a closer look at his "new wheels", and as he explained to me how much his two-wheeler meant to him, he even lovingly ran his hand along the handlebars, which were the type found on racing bicycles: they dropped and curved back in on themselves. My disgust was radically heightened due to the moderately inebriated state I was in, and I politely but brusquely told him how nice I thought it was, hoping the faux compliments would be enough to set him on his way.

But it didn't work. He stayed and asked whether I would like to take it for a ride, to see how "smooth she was", all the while giggling like a schoolgirl who was in the process of being asked to the movies by the man of her dreams. I quickly declined his insincere offer, but he still wouldn't move; He could sense my undiminished frustration, and began to childishly taunt me, suggesting that I wouldn't know how to ride his bike properly, anyway.

At that point I think I finally lost control.

The whisky had instilled me with enough raw confidence to show him he was wrong. I inelegantly shoved him aside, his mouth agape. He lost his grip on his metal-framed companion, but I expertly caught it, leapt onto it, and then pedalled ferociously. His precious contraption moved forward with surprising ease, and the air was soon brushing past me, taking with it my cares. I soared down the road, my eyes barely open, happiness washing over me. He was right: it was pretty smooth.

I didn't notice the rickshaw until the very last moment, and there was nothing I could have done to avoid a collision – I ploughed into its side, causing a bone-crunching rattle. The passenger, an elderly lady, was shouting obscenities and trying to teach me some sort of lesson with the aid of her walking stick. Deflecting her weak blows like a mentally deficient trainee ninja, I tried to pull the bicycle away, but one of its hooked handlebars was caught in the frame of the rickshaw; all I did was drag everything along the road by a few miserable feet. The astonished owner of the rickshaw stared at me with a lifeless, flummoxed look on his face, and for some reason, my only thought was that strangely, it suited him.

After a few more ineffectual tugs of the bicycle, by which time a group of excited onlookers had congregated, the inner workings of my exhausted brain were up and running again; I carefully unhooked the handlebar from the rickshaw.

After freeing it I slowly walked back, red faced, past the tittering crowd and towards the lanky boy, who stood horrified ahead of me – his jaw dangling from his stunned face in complete concern for his bicycle. Before I could reach him, a small youngster ran to me and tugged at my arm. He looked at me with a sad and innocent expression, and it seemed as though he genuinely cared for my well-being. His eyes widened and welled up slightly as he opened his diminutive mouth to speak, and the gathered crowd hushed in order to hear what this tiny, fragile-looking boy wanted to say. I waited for words of consolation and grief, but with one sentence he restored the situation to its former hilarity.

"Can't you ride a bike yet?"

Squiggle

On that particular Thursday, I became tired of work earlier than usual, and decided to head for home. It was a bright summer afternoon, and it made a pleasant change to avoid the traditional rush-hour tube huddle[23]. In fact, before I knew it, I had reached my station.

Walking home after the brief journey, I was momentarily distracted by what looked like a small bundle of brown-grey fur at the foot of a tree. Approaching it, I noticed that it was slowly stirring, and upon reaching it, I realised that it was actually two baby squirrels. However my mood was suddenly dampened; I noticed that one of the pair was covered in blood, clearly lifeless. The other was standing by its deceased acquaintance, sniffing the corpse as squalid flies buzzed about unceremoniously.

Altogether dumbstruck, I froze, considering what to do next. I knelt down and regarded the despondently inquisitive squirrel; it repeatedly prodded its companion with its nose, trying to revive it. I instinctively put out my hand, not knowing what to expect, and it stopped what it was doing and looked at me, its large, dark, reflective eyes covered in a thin, watery film.

Edging my hand closer, I observed intently as the young squirrel inched cautiously towards it, smelling my skin. It approached my palm and lifted one of its front paws onto it, and I realised that I had never noticed how much a squirrel's paws resembled miniature, furry human hands. Instinctively, I lowered my hand further, until it was resting on the warm pavement, and that was when the squirrel did something that will forever remain with me.

It slowly crept onto my palm, and then put its head down and closed its eyes. Carefully standing up, as it gently breathed against my skin, I took a final look at its dead compatriot, and resolved what to do; my journey home commenced, the pace slowed somewhat, with the squirrel resting safely in my hand.

En route I covertly determined that it was male, and immediately decided on a name for my new friend: Squiggle.

Upon my arrival, I found a large shoebox and placed into it a small but varied selection of nuts. I made a makeshift bed using a dishcloth, and then unhurriedly placed Squiggle inside. He rested, while I readied a saucer of water. After making sure he had everything he might need, he was left to recuperate. I had already decided whom to call for help: The Royal Society for the Prevention of Cruelty to Animals; It was clear to me that the RSPCA would be able to give Squiggle a lot more care and attention, so I called them to find out when they could come and collect him.

They weren't able to come around for a couple of days, as they were short of staff, but we did manage to arrange a convenient time, after which I decided to have something for dinner.

Following my meal, I went to check up on Squiggle; he was awake, inspecting his new home. I gently lifted him up and held him in my hand. I hadn't noticed earlier how his tiny eyes barely looked open, and I smiled whilst twirling my finger around his tail: he was so young it hadn't yet attained its trademark bushiness.

As he lay in my hand, his head moving about aimlessly, he yawned, showing thin but perfectly formed teeth. He began to gnaw gently on my finger, his jaw not wide enough to grip any sizable chunk of my finger; his miniature teeth tickled me as they brushed across my skin.

I was captivated by his innocence and held him for some time as he wandered up and down my arm, trying to chew it in various places along the way but only succeeding in tickling me further. After a few minutes he grew tired and I put him back into his box, which was near my bed, and left him in peace while I continued my evening.

Soon it was time to get some sleep, but I first checked on Squiggle. He was asleep; I could see his fuzzy belly rising and falling as he breathed delicately. I sighed, remembering his deceased playmate. I thought back, wondering if I should have picked it up too, and given it a proper burial. Perhaps if I weren't so taken aback by the affecting situation I would have had the foresight to do so.

As I lay in bed that night, bittersweet feelings passed through my deliberating mind. I wondered whether the other squirrel was Squiggle's sibling, mulled over how old Squiggle was, and imagined what Squiggle would say if he could speak. Whilst waiting for slumber to pass over me, my thoughts slowly became more and more pleasant, and eventually, I drifted away...

I woke with a start. My senses were invaded by a shrill screeching and the sound of cardboard rustling. The alarm clock slowly came into focus: it was not yet 6am. I got out of bed to investigate; it was Squiggle, running manically around in his box and calling out to me; he was probably hungry. I picked him up and took him with me to get some more nuts and water. Afterwards, he went back into his box and immediately quietened down before nibbling attentively on a walnut.

I toyed with the idea of calling in sick, but ultimately resolved that it was probably a good idea to turn up for work as normal – I had been slacking quite comprehensively of late. So it was with a heavy heart that I left Squiggle alone and started my journey to the office. The day wore on, and ironically its highlights were all conversations with my colleagues about my new friend.

Before I knew it, it was time to head for home, but when I finally got there, I noticed something was amiss: Squiggle wasn't in his box. I stood there in silence and disbelief, in an attempt to deduce what could have happened. Bar the walnuts, half of the food was left in the box, but there was no sign of Squiggle. I frantically inspected the room, my every thought hijacked by worry, when my eyes fell upon a peculiar sight: the bed had a small lump in the blanket; it looked as though there was something under it.

I conscientiously lifted it, and my anxiousness melted into delight; Squiggle was lying there, asleep, breathing peacefully. Carefully replacing the blanket, I smiled to myself; I even caught myself giggling as I walked to the kitchen to make a cup of tea, picturing in my mind the baby squirrel escaping from the box and discovering the refuge of the warm bed.

My routine that evening was virtually identical to that of the night before, and I found myself becoming attached to Squiggle; though a pang of sadness passed through me each time I remembered he would be leaving the next day.

That night, I mused as I tried to get to sleep. Would a squirrel make a good pet? Would it be fair? What would the squirrel want? Altogether exhausted, I finally flittered into a dream...

The next morning, Squiggle woke me up in precisely the same way, at a similarly early hour. Under normal circumstances, this was something that had the potential to greatly annoy me, but for Squiggle I made an exception. I got up and looked at him running around in his box. Knowing he would be leaving that day, I exhaled dramatically.

The morning continued in a similar vein to that of the day before, except it was Saturday: I didn't need to go to work. Instead, I sat with Squiggle for a few hours, while he ran around, chewed on things, and generally caused mischief, until I heard the doorbell ring.

It was a man from the RSPCA, who for some reason spoke in an exceedingly grave voice, like a policeman passing on the death message. He told me that collecting squirrels was not common procedure, but that they couldn't just ignore my call.

I introduced him to Squiggle, and the man was instantly taken with him. He knew how to make the squirrel feel comfortable. I could see that Squiggle was in good hands, literally.

The man listened intently as he was told the full story, but then it was time for Squiggle to go. It was a moment I had been anticipating with sadness, and when it inescapably arrived, confusion rattled through me. I looked at Squiggle, his little ears twitching, before lifting him and stroking his back for a few minutes, saying my goodbyes. I furtively noticed the man from the RSPCA watching me as though he was looking at a sufferer of acute dementia.

Then it was time to go. The man carried Squiggle back to his van, and I waved as they slowly drove away. I remained there in the doorway for a few minutes, looking out into the street. I contemplated whether Squiggle would be safe and also whether he would ever live a normal life.

It started to rain, so I went back inside and made myself a cup of tea. The place suddenly felt barren. I pondered what to do over the rest of the weekend. It was different without Squiggle. Subsequently, I came up with some menial chores to take my mind off things, and tried to continue my day with as much normality as I could muster. The weekend passed routinely, and so did the days that followed.

But I would always remember the diminutive squirrel that injected my summer with adventure and drama.

I would never forget Squiggle.

Country and western

Dolly Parton's voice blared through the speakers as I waited patiently at the bar, trying to deduce exactly how Willie had coerced me into going along with him. The girl being served was wearing cowboy boots and a straw hat. I asked myself again: what I was doing there?

I glanced at Willie; he was surrounded by appropriately attired bodies: stonewashed denim, worn leather and jangling belt buckles. They were laughing, joking and dancing; if there was one thing Willie was good at, it was the ability to talk his way into any clique.

Bringing the drinks over, I regarded the people we had met that evening; they all seemed friendly enough - I had already spoken to some of them and they displayed none of the 'attitude' commonly associated with Londoners. Willie was talking to an older lady whose face, for some reason, conjured up images in my mind, though not in an excessively adverse way, of a spider monkey[24].

The party continued, and as more and more drinks arrived, the country and western songs melted into what, to me, was an unrecognisable cacophony. It seemed, looking around, that I was one of very few people there unfamiliar with the music. Still, I was having a good time, and so was Willie, judging by the indestructible smirk bound to his face.

Willie introduced me to Kensal, the older lady, and we talked at length, about nothing in particular. She was the focal point of their group, and was very popular; speaking to her was not unpleasant, even with the constant interruptions by her friends: photo requests, drink orders and greetings.

The drinks flowed further, and as the night progressed, the dance floor steadily evolved into a heaving blur of checked shirts and Stetsons, moving approximately to the rhythm of Kenny Rogers' down-tuned guitar.

11pm arrived, and, pub-licensing hours being what they were, so did the end of the party; though I enjoyed it substantially more than I had expected to. Our collection of untiring reprobates was buzzing, and we fervently deliberated over other venues to move on to; it was Friday, and the night was still in bloom.

After staggering through the forgotten streets of Farringdon in the rain for many minutes and not getting any closer to deciding where to go[25], an invisible light bulb shimmered above Kensal's head, and she made a unique and promising suggestion: she worked nearby and had the keys to her office. There were refreshments there too, as well as ample music, apparently. This idea was a resounding success amongst our number, and we cheerfully trudged through the puddles on the pavement as she triumphantly led the way.

A few minutes later, Kensal unlocked a door and we followed her up a flight of dark, echoing stairs. At the top, she sauntered through a doorway and flicked a switch. As the lights came alive one by one, the surroundings gradually became discernible.

We were in awe as we entered room – it looked more like a luxury apartment than an office; there was a leather sofa which overlooked a large television set and opulent sound system, a dining area surrounded by framed portraits, and a kitchen that looked like an expensive showroom installation. Though, I couldn't spot where anyone actually worked: there were no desks or computers anywhere to be seen.

Kensal lifted a plush bottle of Champagne from the fridge and popped it open, before pouring everyone a crystal glassful. We clinked glasses and sipped our drinks whilst we made small talk and listened to the music emanating from the Bose hi-fi.

The bottle had soon been depleted, and Kensal indifferently plucked another from the refrigerator. Whilst she wrestled with the plastic that covered the cork, I asked her if she could tell me where the toilets were located. She explained whilst pointing to a corridor I hadn't noticed before; I didn't quite grasp her directions, but fearlessly ventured forth nonetheless.

As I stepped into the corridor, the lights automatically awakened; movement sensors, I concluded, as I noticed a series of indistinguishable, smart wooden doors, all unmarked and windowless – the toilet could have been behind any one of them. I tussled with the urge to return and ask for the directions again, though I finally resisted; I wanted to find it on my own.

Approaching the first door, I hesitated; what if it was the wrong door? What if there was someone inside? Swallowing my doubts, I turned the handle and pushed. The light bulb fizzed into life; it was a small but stylish office, with a desk, PC, and sofa bed, which had been prepared for someone to go to sleep in. I ticked off one of the outstanding checkboxes on my cerebral to-do list: I had found a room in the building where it was possible to do some actual work.

I let the door swing shut and walked to the next; in its unopened state, it was identical. However, upon entering, I was struck with a pang of disappointment: I had found the room I was looking for, sooner than expected. I entered with an audible groan and locked the door behind me.

Upon my exit, I probably smelled better: I had taken advantage of the expensive eau de Cologne on display by the glossy white ceramic sink. But at that point I was faced with a dilemma: should I explore the remainder of the building by myself, or should I return for Willie?

Back in the kitchen area, I found him, barely able to stand, precariously pouring another drink. I retrieved my glass and told him to come with me: I wanted to show him something. He obediently began to follow, continuing to waywardly fill his glass from the bottle he brought with him.

To say that Willie was amazed when he saw the corridor, with its multitude of doors, is an understatement; however, I put much of this down to his severely intoxicated state. After seeing the first two rooms, his enthusiasm massively outweighed mine. So, together, we tried the third door.

We were not disappointed.

As we entered, our jaws hung limply from our faces and our eyes popped from their sockets in wonder. The many lights came alive one by one and with each, our childlike astonishment increased further.

It was a massive chamber – even larger than the main room – and had wood panelled walls covered with framed paintings, the significance of which eluded us. There were glass cabinets situated at regular intervals, and, examining those in our proximity, we discovered they were filled with intricate scale models of various buildings and boats.

We looked at each other and simultaneously burst into uncontrollable laughter, which continued for many minutes. Then, gulping down our drinks, we walked around the room, discussing the various miniatures. Periodically, Willie would notice that one of our glasses was nearing emptiness and would robotically refill it.

The more cabinets we inspected, the harder it became for us to deduce what they all had in common; we saw many elaborately designed buildings, all of which were modern-looking and grand. There were also many seafaring vessels: ocean liners, yachts and speedboats, as well as other types of boat that were not immediately familiar to either one of us.

Ambling around the room, talking and laughing, we finished the contents of the bottle. I looked at Willie; he looked as drunk as I had ever seen him. Glancing at my wristwatch, I paused until my eyes could focus on the hands.

It took a few seconds but I could see that it was almost 4am. Willie was visibly disturbed by this and insisted that we leave immediately.

We returned to the main room, where Willie picked up a lavish, unopened bottle of vintage wine and pretended to fascinatedly examine its label. He gave me a wink before announcing that he was going to use the lavatory, and then hobbled away holding the bottle in such a way that his body obscured it.

I exhaled sharply. Willie, when in an uninhibited state, did some bizarre things, and I never quite knew what to expect. As I waited for his return, I interrupted Kensal, who by then was firmly in the process of striking it lucky with one of the guys in the group. I thanked her for her hospitality and explained that we needed to leave; she seemed sad that we were going but was glad that we came along.

Willie returned, doubled over, and declared that he had had far too much to drink and was feeling very ill. It was incredibly obvious to me where he had hidden the bottle, and I tried to determine whether anyone else would arrive at the same conclusion. He waddled over to the staircase, where I waited with Kensal, and he waved goodbye to her.

She gave me a goodbye hug, and then looked at Willie. His eyes opened wide and he started for the staircase, but Kensal put her hand onto his arm and asked where her hug was.

I instinctively put my hand to my mouth, fearing she would discover the bottle, as she put her arms around his hunched frame and hugged him tightly. I watched in fright as she gave him a peck on the cheek and then said goodbye. As she pulled away, relief overcame me, and I made my way down the dark stairs. Willie followed, and a short while later, we were outside the building.

Outside, Willie extracted the bottle from the front of his trousers and murmured incoherently. I held my head in my hands as he garbled a victory cheer and then released a burp. Then he simply sat on the pavement, holding his prize, smirking; the escapade seemed to have drained him of all energy. He looked at me and begged me to make sure he got home safely; I could always sleep on the couch, he added.

I assented, and stood by the side of the silent, barren road, waiting for a taxi to go past. Eventually one arrived and reluctantly agreed to take us to Primrose Hill. We got in and the cab lurched forward furiously; Willie grimaced in the manner of a man edging closer to the unenviable state in which he would need to violently disgorge.

"Excuse me, driver? Sorry to bother you, but could you pull over for a second, please? I need to be ill", Willie slurred a few minutes into our journey[26].

The car quickly ground to a halt and the driver and I looked at Willie, expectantly.

"Sorry, false alarm. Please continue, driver. Apologies."

The driver turned back around, emotionless, and the cab gained speed. I grinned at Willie as he caressed his wine bottle, completely oblivious to everything else.

Much to the chagrin of the driver, Willie repeated the same trick twice during the short drive, and for a time also could not recall where he lived.

We got out of the taxi and staggered up the short cul-de-sac to Willie's flat. As soon as we got inside, I took my shoes off and fell onto the larger of the two couches. It was nice to finally relax, despite the fact that everything was slowly spinning.

Willie left my line of sight and returned a short while later with a blanket, which he absently threw towards me before leaving again. I arranged my limbs until I was in a comfortable position, and then allowed my heavy eyelids to close.

Just as my brain was beginning to shut down for the night, I was woken by Willie's voice. I silently stood up and crept to his doorway. He was sitting cross-legged on the floor flicking through his country and western vinyl collection. Every now and again he would pause to meticulously examine a particular record. Finally, he took one from its sleeve and placed it on the turntable, before carefully placing the stylus into the groove; he then began to speak.

"Thanks, everybody, for coming tonight – it's great to be here. Here's a nice upbeat ditty to get things moving."

The song began. I simply shook my head in disbelief; what was he doing? I crept back to the sofa and tried to get some sleep. With lyrics about gambling debts and broken hearts running through my groggy mind, I fell asleep...

I was woken with a start. It was dark, and it took my eyes a short while to become accustomed to the lack of light. I could just make out Willie, standing in the corner of the room, facing the wall, saying something; however the more I tried to decipher his words, the more I realised that he was talking gibberish. I finally gave up and put my head under the blanket in another attempt to return to the land of sleep.

A few moments later, he was silent.

I lifted my head and glanced at him. He had stopped talking, and had turned to face the couch. He blindly shuffled towards me, and it was only when he was a few feet away that I realised that he was completely naked from the waist down. Upon reaching the sofa, he lifted the blanket, got into a comfortable position beside me, and then was still.

Something started to bother me, though I couldn't quite put my finger on it.

A few minutes later, he was snoring contentedly; I still had the sense that something was wrong, though it was a few further minutes before I, in my inebriated state, realised what was unusual about the situation.

Quietly, and still in no condition to be able to be completely certain that anything out of the ordinary had actually taken place, I climbed onto the back of the sofa, crawled to the end, and dropped onto the carpet. I looked at Willie and groaned. I padded to his bedroom, took his blanket and collapsed onto the other sofa.

The sun had begun to rise, and my exhausted body had little problem falling into slumber.

Morning duly arrived, and Willie was wide-awake, his face stricken with bewilderment.

"What on earth am I doing on the sofa?" He asked.

I shrugged, and was about to attempt some sort of explanation, when he lifted the blanket and inspected himself. He looked at me in horror.

"And where the hell are my pants?!"

My head dropped back onto the sofa and I sighed, as Willie walked towards the bathroom, the blanket sparing his blushes.

I turned to one side and caught a glimpse of the vintage wine bottle on the coffee table. Little did he know, but three days later, Willie would give it away to an attractive girl at a bar, in return for her phone number.

Unfortunately, even before getting back home, he would lose it.

Double-bill

The best thing about Mondays was getting to write about what happened over the weekend. Though I was only eleven years old, I had realised that there was no real way for the teacher to actually verify the authenticity of these stories, and thus they had progressively become more and more implausible.

As Mr. O'Malley read about the red Lamborghini Countach that had been donated to me by a complete stranger purely as reward for my unflinching kindness, I looked forward with excitement to the afternoon: after lunch, our class was going to visit the nearby high school to create a mural from mosaics, and I couldn't wait.

Soon it was time for our morning break, and I rushed with my friends into the sun-baked playground to catch up after the weekend. We chatted about the hugely exciting episode of The A-Team[27] that was aired on Saturday, the highlight of which, we unanimously agreed, was a scene where a taxi cab, driven by 'B.A.' Baracus[28], careered dangerously through busy streets at extremely high speed. As we discussed the finer points of the scene, something on the ground caught my eye.

I looked down to discover a crane fly – though *daddy longlegs* was the name generally used in the playground – and a wasp, locked in battle. It was immediately clear to me that the crane fly, with its spindly legs and slender abdomen, was likely to come off worse. I crouched to get a closer look.

The wasp gripped the crane fly in a headlock and was punching it repeatedly in the head; the crane fly tried to block these blows with its delicate legs, but the wasp was agile; it timed its onslaught such that the vast majority of its jabs caught the crane fly's tiny snout. The wasp was toying with it; in fact, the crane fly was an inept brawler and wasn't even fighting back. Instead it just grimaced, its face covered in miniature bruises, and screamed for the wasp to stop.

Snapping from my fantasia, I noticed that there was a group of children circling the action. Gusts of wind blew the combatants around in random directions, and our ring of juveniles veered and stretched in order to maintain a good view of the duel.

Soon, though, the altercation turned nasty. The wasp knew it could overpower its opponent at any time, and when it finally decided to, there were devastating consequences: it effortlessly tore a leg from the crane fly and watched it drift away in the breeze. The fighters rolled around some more, air currents buffeting their tiny bodies, and soon another limb had gone the way of the first.

One by one, the wasp ripped the legs from the crane fly and left them to the elements. Each was accompanied by a silent shriek, as the crane fly was slowly maimed. Its wings followed in the same manner, and glinted wildly as they were tossed into the wind. And then, the fight was over. The crane fly's limbless abdomen twitched erratically as the wasp danced victoriously over it.

By the time the teacher arrived to see what we were all looking at, the wasp had concluded its celebrations and flown away; all that remained was the limbless and motionless corpse of the crane fly. The teacher was convinced that she had just missed some sort of ritualistic insect sacrifice, and no amount of pleading on our part appeased her. During her extensive reprimand, the buzzer sounded to signify the end of break; it was time to head back to the classroom.

The remainder of the morning went quickly: we were all overexcited about the wasp, as well as the forthcoming trip to create the mural, and before long, it was lunchtime.

Over the lunch break, we decided to play football, and during the course of the largely uneventful game, I noticed Goebbels, the stocky loner. He was sitting on the floor beside one of the wooden benches we were using as a goal, scratching randomly at it using a small sharp stone that had been selected from a pile he gathered earlier.

Every so often Goebbels looked among us, his eyes burning with contempt and hate. Whenever someone neared him, Goebbels would hurl one of his stones in the general direction of whoever it was, and, more often than not, he managed to hit his intended target.

Soon, it was my turn to become his victim. Running up the right wing, I cut inside and launched a good cross into the area, but then immediately felt a sharp pain on my cheek. Instinctively, my hand jerked up to check my face, and I turned to look at Goebbels. He was gazing directly at me, his face showing nothing but anger. He awkwardly got to his feet and rapidly flicked another stone at me. I stood there, dumbfounded, as it hit me in the cheek again, in almost exactly the same spot. I considered whether he had been practising.

My disorientation slowly turned into infuriation, and I approached him, incensed. What gave him the right to behave in that way? I got nearer, realising that I didn't actually have a plan: I had no idea what I was going to say or do when I reached him; though he was a lot bigger than me, so violence was out of the question.

As I got within a few feet of him, he turned his body, lifted his leg, and swung it towards me. I evaded this clumsy kick, and as his momentum carried him off balance, I changed my mind: I wanted to fight back. I wanted to hurt him; he deserved it. I aimed a fist at his head. It struck him straight on the nose, and he reeled in bewilderment; he probably expected very little in the way of retaliation.

He attempted his kick again and this time it connected with my leg. I don't know whether it was my rage, or simply that it was a poor effort on his part, but I felt no pain. Instead, I punched him in the nose again, and he careened backwards, swaying in confusion.

At that point, everything else ceased to exist; it was just the two of us, locked in battle.

I was consumed by frenzy, and it seemed as though I had turned the tables upon my inadequate antagonist. He was using his arms to try and shield his face from my barrage of punches, but I found it increasingly easy to make contact with his skull. I abhorred violence – I still do – but there was a strange satisfaction in causing him pain. Eventually, he was squatting, arms above his head, crying, begging me to stop.

That was when the teacher arrived. She broke up the scuffle and sent me to see the headmaster. As I walked away, I could hear the other children; they were staunchly defending me, explaining that I hadn't been the one to start the fight.

It was quieter in the building, and as I walked, melancholy descended upon me. I didn't want to hurt anyone – not really. But I had to, didn't I? If I didn't fight back, wouldn't he have just hurt me instead? I thought of the crane fly; I wondered whether there had ever been one that, upon being attacked by a wasp, fought back. What would the wasp have thought? Would it have just given up?

Whilst waiting outside the headmaster's office, I looked at my hand, and was horrified to find that it was shaking violently. My breathing was unnatural and a queasy feeling had infested the pit of my stomach. I sat there, thinking; trying to work out whether there was some other way I could have handled the situation. Was I in trouble? If so, it hardly seemed fair to me.

Soon it was time to go in, and as I saw the headmaster, I reflected; the children found him a constant source of amusement. He probably thought it was because he tried to empathise with them – he also often began bizarre and completely irrelevant conversations with them – but I knew the real reason was simply because he bore an uncanny resemblance to the bad guy from *Robocop*[29]. I usually snickered involuntarily at the mere sight of him, but I felt so unhappy about the way the day was going that I couldn't even muster a happy thought, let alone a smile.

We chatted for some time, and after hearing my story, he told me that he was of the opinion that I acted in self-defence. Satisfied that this was the case, he began to talk about Sudanese Neolithic figurines and the parallels they have with Egyptian figurines from the same era. This bombardment of data was, however, lost on me, and I left his office feeling more fatigued, mentally, than when I went in.

I miserably traipsed slowly back to the classroom, in a world of my own. I thought about the fight and the effect it had had on my state of mind. I worried about what the other children might think of me.

My ponderings were interrupted by a teacher who wore a slightly perturbed look. She told me that lunch had ended a while ago and that Mr. O'Malley had been searching for me. As I had been nowhere to be seen, the rest of the class had left without me.

Damn. The trip to create the mosaic. I had completely forgotten.

Everything finally caught up with me. Deflated and with a sense of rejection, I burst hysterically into tears. The teacher stared at me, unaware of the sequence of events that had led to the loud sobbing she was witnessing: to her this must have seemed like a massive overreaction. As she tried to work out what to do next, I whimpered and bawled, wondering if, somewhere, there was a crane fly doing the exact same thing.

The unexpected shadow

After absently flicking through all four channels on the television, I reluctantly decided to watch *New Faces of 86*, a programme aimed at showcasing new and varied talent, most of which seemed to be an excuse to point and laugh at people who had little or no aptitude. It wasn't that I really wanted to watch it, but there wasn't much else in the way of entertainment on that Saturday evening.

I was almost eight years old. And I was home alone again. Things were different in those days though; it was perfectly acceptable, and fairly common, to allow youngsters to look after themselves.

I got up to close the curtains, as a Chinese acrobatic troupe formed, to rapturous applause, a precarious 3 dimensional scale representation of a Volkswagen Beetle. It was already dark, and there was a noticeable chill in the air.

After returning to the sofa, I leafed through the book on origami that I had borrowed from the library a few years prior, incredibly pleased to have finally made time to read it. I was part way through putting together a 17-piece living room furniture set; I'd followed the alarmingly precise instructions as closely as I could. So far I had finished the television and its stand, but had a long way to go before the rest of the items – the chairs, tables, cabinets, VHS recorder and basic cutlery – would be complete. Methodically, I continued working through the pages, robotically completing the tasks, but I soon realised that further sheets of paper were required.

Getting to my feet, I strolled through the kitchen, and the hallway following it, to the back of the flat, where there was a room in which all manner of miscellany was kept. Rummaging around, I gathered a few sheets of paper; there were also some crayons, which I decided to take with me in case my creation required any final touches.

As I was about to leave the room, however, I saw something that made me stop in the doorway, struck with confusion: there was a shadow on the wall of the adjacent room. It had the shape of a person, and at first glance, I could not tell whether it was cast by me. I waggled my right arm considerably, but the shadow's arms both remained static. I froze in horror, morbid visions beginning to hatch from imaginary eggs that were kept inside my skull.

If it wasn't my shadow, then whose was it? I wondered whether I was the victim of a prank – that someone was lying in wait to jump out and scare me – but just as I began to compile a mental list of suspects, I saw the top of the culprit's head peek out from behind the door. My heart started pumping faster: though his face was bathed in shadow, I could see he was a stranger. He stared at me with eyes that were filled with anger – the same look I often received from most of my schoolteachers.

An intense fear tore through my body, and questions raced through my mind. Who was he, and what was he doing in the flat? How did he get in? Had I interrupted him? What would he to do me if I got in his way? I'm slightly ashamed to say that a shiver worked its way through me.

His eyes seemed then to be so bright that everything else faded into obscurity. He stared at me as though trying to comprehend why he was watching a small child gaping incessantly at him.

I had a flashback: a nature documentary. A deer stumbled upon a tiger in dense jungle. Instead of immediately running away, it simply stared into the tiger's eyes. Then, a few seconds later, it bolted with the tiger in close pursuit.

I turned and ran through the hallway towards the living room. From the television I could hear what sounded like *Lady in Red* being played and sung by a group of tone-deaf pensioners who between them had never even seen a piano, let alone been permitted to touch one. I pushed the grisly fate of the deer from my thoughts, and just ran without looking back. The paper and crayons fell from my hands as I made my way back into the living room.

Once there, I grabbed the telephone from the table, and hid underneath it (the table), taking it (the telephone) with me. My stomach was doing somersaults and I couldn't work out whether this was caused by fear or simply the elderly whimpering coming from the television set.

Picking up the handset, I waited impatiently for the tone, and then dialled the number for my father's place of work. The clicks and whirrs seemed to be taking longer than usual, but eventually it began to ring. After a couple of rings, he answered.

"There's someone in the house," I whispered.

"I'm on my way!" he yelled, anguish evident in his voice.

He worked not far away and under normal circumstances the journey could be made in a few minutes. I sat there in silence, trying not to make any noise as I waited for him under the table.

The wait seemed to last forever. I began to hear noises, and, though I was sure these were a figment of my imagination, I was gripped by fear. I could hear someone stomping around in the flat, slamming doors. Or could I? Perhaps it was all in my head?

However, I would never find out, because as my fright reached its pinnacle, the noises stopped. And at that exact moment, the front door burst open and my father stepped into sight.

The anxiety drained from my system and I ran to him in relief. I told him what I'd seen, and he instructed me to follow close behind him. He went into the kitchen and picked up the largest frying pan he could find, before continuing through the hallway and into the master bedroom.

The place was a mess; most of the wardrobes, cupboards and drawers were open, and their contents spilled out onto the floor; there was, however, no sign of the man I had seen. My father looked at me, bewildered, and I could see in his eyes the faint suspicion that this was all my doing. I wondered what this said about me as a child, and vowed to review the situation after the conclusion of this episode.

But wait.

Maybe he was right? I had hallucinated once or twice. I suffered the occasional spell of sleepwalking. Amnesia haunted me. As I thought about it, I began to doubt my own conviction; the mess in the room could easily have been caused by me. And the peeking head? The noises? Imaginary. Perhaps it was my doing, after all?

It was with my head hung low that I followed my father into my room. Once inside though, I breathed a sigh of relief: the window had been prised open and that there was a giant dirty footprint on the bed. My suspicions – as well as his – were put to rest. We checked the rest of the flat, but there was no trace; the intruder must have fled.

My mother soon arrived and after seeing the mess in the room, looked accusingly at me. But upon seeing the other evidence, her concern vanished. She was, however, dismayed to find her favourite ring was missing. It contained a ruby and, in the end, was the only item recorded as missing in the police report: everything else had been accounted for.

In time, the insurance covered the value of the ring, but as a replacement, my mother opted for one with a green gem that I decided must have been an emerald.

I, however, took some time to recover. I wished that there were an easy way to heal mental scars. For some days I was too scared to sleep in the flat and had to stay with relatives. For many months I heard noises when alone in the flat, and my father suffered many false alarms. I often woke covered in sweat after experiencing nightmares. My bed-wetting resurfaced, along with my nervous twitches. I often looked back and wished I had been elsewhere on that night.

About six months after the burglary, by which time I would be almost back to normal, I'd be at home on my own again, making a technically exact Supermarine Spitfire solely out of paper, glue and small pieces of scrap metal I had found lying around the home.

Upon its completion, I would throw it and watch it float gracefully across the room, only to land with an elegant patter on top of a wardrobe, before gently falling behind it.

I'd frown, before contorting my frame around the wardrobe to be able to reach it.

After picking it up, I'd see something which would cause me to laugh out loud: a glistening ring, adorned with a solitary stone.

And what would its colour be?

Well, let's just say it wouldn't be green.

The chocolate binge

Inserting a twenty pence piece into the wall-mounted contraption, I diligently inspected the little plastic eggs through the glass. I could never truly decide which one I wanted, and was usually dismayed at what actually came out. The coin bounced jauntily around before ending its journey with a satisfying thump. I turned the giant plastic knob until the device emitted a grinding rattle followed by a solitary clink. My prize awaited.

Eagerly, I pushed open the tiny metal flap and retrieved the egg; it sat there all alone like a brand new toy, waiting to be played with. After picking it up, however, my heart sank.

"Why me?" I cried aloud in frustration as passers by pretended not to notice.

The egg was semi-opaque, and though it was not possible to see exactly what was inside, it was clear to me I wasn't going to be pleased with its contents: it looked as though it contained a chain or a bracelet. What on earth would I do with either of those?

I opened the plastic egg with the defeated groan of an old man on his deathbed who, in addition to being about to expire, had lived a long, arduous life and, at practically every stage, had been severely wronged by almost everyone he knew.

The contents of the egg confirmed my suspicions: it was a simple chain – gold in colour. I knew, however, that it could not actually be made of gold, despite the fact that I was only seven.

Casting the chain into my jacket pocket and trying to forget about it, I began to head for home. Chuckling, I put the empty halves of the egg back together, safe in the knowledge that I could have exponentially more fun with the egg than any chain, gold or not.

I arrived home at teatime and was fairly excited about being given a KitKat to have with my tea. Something I did after receiving one was save a stick or two. I'd hide them behind the television set when nobody was looking and then every now and again, when the house was empty, I'd initiate what I liked to call *the chocolate binge*, which basically involved gorging myself on the stuff. I have come to understand that my family knew exactly what was going on, and gained their own amusement from keeping track of the hidden chocolate bars. It has since become apparent that they even had some kind of sweepstake going.

Three of the sticks I enjoyed with my cup of tea, the other went into the pile behind the TV, which was beginning to build up quite nicely.

The evening progressed in an orderly fashion and I was unable to distinguish it from most others from that era: television, dinner, bed.

At school, the next day, I was distraught to find that my teacher was unable to spell the word *astronaut*, even though my story *Killer astronaut from Mars*[30] actually utilised the correct spelling at least fifteen times. It was about an astronaut from the future who had been part of a government initiative to colonise the moon, only to be betrayed by his countrymen and left for dead on Mars. Of course, he actually survived, and, in fact, had gained an amazing, but horrifying, superpower: the ability to kill anything just by thinking about it. The story charted the breathtaking highs and the stooping lows of his life, and I was actually incredibly proud of it. It upset me that the teacher had defaced it with reams of false accusations.

Entranced, I looked over at Dusty, the girl of my dreams. She was sitting next to her best friend, Victoria, probably talking about girl things. I didn't understand these bizarre creatures, but hoped to, one day.

It was soon time to go to the canteen, but before we left we needed to tidy our desks. We put our books and pencils into our trays and then returned the trays to their places in the rack against the wall; this was to keep our desks tidy, I inferred. I regularly mused about the origin of these trays. Who invented them? And what had this genius gone on to achieve?[31]

After eating almost half of my poor excuse for a meal, I put my hand into my pocket; it brushed against something that I had forgotten about: the chain.

The tiny embryo of a plan slowly emerged from somewhere inside my brain. I nurtured and fed it until it was ready to be thrust into the big, scary world, at which point I suspected it would probably turn on me wildly. The plan was a simple one: give the chain to Dusty along with an exquisitely written note declaring my affection. How could that fail to make her mine?

So, after giving up on lunch, I began to scrawl onto a piece of scrap paper I found in my pocket.

Dear Dusty,

I like you lots.

I got you a necklace. I hope you like it. It's not really gold, but it looks like quite nice.

I wish I could sit next to you.

Do you like me?

I signed it, and read over it. Something wasn't right with it. After lengthy deliberation, I made a small addition.

P.S. Please don't tell anyone about this.

I made an envelope from another piece of scrap paper and placed the chain and the note inside. Perfect. It couldn't go wrong. Now there was only one problem: I was too scared to just go up and hand it to her.

But, ever the problem-solver, I swiftly came up with a solution: I'd simply put it into her tray when it was in the rack. She would go and collect it, be bowled over by the note, wowed by the chain, and come running into my arms. Easy.

Back in the classroom that afternoon, it felt as though butterflies were learning to swim in my stomach. When the teacher requested us to collect our trays, I jumped to my feet and was the first to arrive at the rack. The tray I was looking for was easy to spot; her name was written on a sticker on its side.

As I walked past it, I discreetly dropped the envelope into it. Phase one complete.

Back at my desk, I sat and observed, as an intense fear tore through me. Dusty and Victoria, virtually inseparable, collected their trays together. My heart was thumping in my chest; I felt uncomfortably hot; my head began to throb.

They sat down, and I watched in alarm as Victoria pointed out the envelope to Dusty.

My symptoms worsened. I really should have seen this coming.

The two of them opened it together and read the note, looking over at me periodically, giggling in confusion.

I didn't know where to look. Victoria was holding the chain up to Dusty's neck to see how it would look. I cringed, realising I should have gone directly to Dusty. Soon the whole class would know about my stupid note.

What was I to do? The only logical course of action, I decided, was to deny everything.

So I blamed Goebbels, the stocky, friendless boy.

Of course, he knew nothing about it, and would say as much, but it would be his word against mine. In all honesty I didn't – and probably never would – know what most of my classmates thought.

The next lesson began, and soon all was put aside, for a little while anyway. I trudged through the hour, trying not to think about my disastrous actions, but I was too distracted by thoughts to be anywhere near productive.

It was in this state that I ended the lesson, not even being able to discern which subject we were being taught.

And then it was time for Physical Education. If anything, I assumed P.E. would take my mind off things; I was quite looking forward to forgetting how moronic I had been.

In those days, it was normal for kids changing for P.E. to do so together, in the classroom, and this is how it was at our school. I started to change, slowly, still distracted by my thoughts. I was now far too scared to talk to Dusty and had no idea of what she thought of the debacle.

As the children finished changing, they marched off to the gym. However after stripping down to my underpants, a nice stripy, almost jubilant pair[32], I noticed the bag containing my shorts and T-shirt wasn't where I had expected it to be.

I glanced around at the classroom, now almost childless, but couldn't see it anywhere. Panic entered my mind, but I tried to remain calm.

Soon, virtually all of my classmates had left for the gym. There were only two of us left: Victoria, and myself.

"Come here, I need to show you something," she called across the room.

Standing there, wearing nothing but my style-defying Y-fronts, I looked across to the other side of the room. Maybe she had found my clothes?

I shuffled over, shivering from the cold, and as I reached the opposite side of the room, I was caught off guard; Victoria grabbed me by the waist and pulled me close.

Instinctively, I closed my eyes, but they were forced open again almost immediately, because I felt something in my mouth. At first I felt disbelief, probably brought on by the shock, but I soon realised that what I was feeling was her tongue.

I pushed away and looked at her.

"I've fancied you for ages," she said, smiling sheepishly.

With immense speed and agility, I simply turned and ran, still wearing virtually nothing.

I looked forward more than anything to getting home that afternoon.

I needed the chocolate binge.

Endnotes

---

[1] A network of caverns and grottos beneath London, which were once inhabited by singing leper-dwarves – known as Cockneys, and now virtually extinct – but are now safe and are used for the purposes of public transport.

[2] Speaking of Euston, most suicides on the London Underground happen at roughly 11am. It is not known why, though, perhaps coincidentally, the Cornish pasty stall at Euston closes at exactly that time for an early lunch.

[3] There are those with the belief that the London Underground transcends the laws of physics. If this is true, then it could be argued that while travelling upon it, the direction to the sky would be impossible to ascertain with any degree of certainty.

[4] It is not my place to judge, but apart from being quite morbidly overweight, he had very poor complexion and an alarming lack of fashion sense. It was clear to me at the time that these issues were directly related to his over-consumption of sugary teatime snacks.

[5] Before UK timescales were reclassified in 1992, it was incredibly difficult to get anything done. Since the reclassification, initiated by John Major and widely considered to be the election clincher, it seems generally as though the wrong sorts of people actually have too much time of their hands; another reclassification has been expected regularly, but has never materialised.

[6] As a child I was fairly resentful of the fact that I had never been fishing. It seemed as though everyone around me was constantly fishing, and, as such, the subject invaded my thoughts regularly.

[7] This is a slight exaggeration, inserted for dramatic effect. It is probably true to say that a schoolteacher would have difficulty getting away with such a thing, even in the eighties, when corporal punishment was still widely used.

[8] Unfortunately, the restaurant no longer exists. I cannot say with any confidence why.

[9] Every year, Australian radio station *Triple J* polls its listeners – composed mostly of self-proclaimed 'trendy' youngsters – and compiles a CD which goes on sale for general consumption. The target market for the CD is predominantly made up of beer-swilling, sailor costume wearing men. No one knows why.

---

[10] Free newspaper given to travellers on the London Underground on a first come, first serve basis. The ink rubs off onto the hands of those that read it, allowing them to be distinguished up to a mile away.

[11] Immense music festival held in the town after which it is named.

[12] It is rumoured that the Wombles once lived in Notting Hill, but were forced by repeated increases in rent to move to Wimbledon. Of course, Uncle Bulgaria, being fairly wealthy, stubbornly acquired a studio flat in Kensington and commuted into the Wimbledon studio every day. His relationship with the other Wombles suffered as a result – it is a common observation that there are often times throughout the show where he seems cold and distant.

[13] Despite being a widely known and accepted fact, scientists are yet to find the connection between camping and prostate cancer. Perhaps in time, as technology advances, they will come to discover the link. For now though, it almost goes without saying: remain vigilant.

[14] Built in 1814, the BBC Micro was years ahead of its time. Unfortunately, the delays to its release (it was unveiled to the general public in 1981) meant that by the time it was available for consumer purchase it was already outdated technology. Today, those still in private ownership are predominantly employed as doorstops and defensive weapons.

[15] They really are very good.

[16] It's also known as *Tramp Juice*, and remains the drink of choice for the homeless in the United Kingdom, probably due to its low price and high alcohol content.

[17] Minor accident treatment centres are fairly unusual, but imagine a small hospital with minimal equipment and staff and you'll probably have a fairly accurate picture in your mind. Better still, suffer a minor accident (or just pretend to) and then visit one.

[18] Of course, I later realised my stupidity: The Incredible Hulk came about because of gamma-radiation.

[19] Unfortunately, this was a short-lived relationship: before my second birthday, I was told that Rover had "run away".

[20] He told me this was common in tall, young, thin men. I'm 5'3" and at the time weighed about 8 stone.

[21] This actually happened.

---

[22] Pickled onion flavoured Monster Munch.

[23] This tradition has fascinated researchers for many years. Upon stepping onto a rush-hour London Underground tube train, mild-mannered, cheerful, respected individuals become irritable, insensitive and insular. Eye-contact is considered physically and morally threatening (identical to behaviour found in gorillas in the wild) and verbal interaction is avoided unless to threaten physical violence. Conversely, physical intimacy is at a maximum: even the most reserved passengers are found with their limbs entwined with those of the (invariably sweaty) folk nearby.

[24] She didn't actually look like a spider monkey, she just reminded me of one. I don't entirely know why.

[25] A strange phenomenon in London: after 11pm it becomes infinitely more difficult to find a drinking establishment that will let you in.

[26] For some reason, Willie is always ultra-courteous to taxi drivers, even those he is not hiring, and especially when he is incredibly drunk.

[27] An 80s Television show featuring a team of mercenaries that could build armoured vehicles and guns from bits of old junk from an old barn. Indeed, they often even did this whilst locked in the barn themselves, prompting the viewer to wonder whether they carried pocket tools.

[28] His first name was actually *Bosco* but I don't remember anyone every having the courage to refer to him in this way.

[29] Classic movie from 1987, in which the government builds a virtually indestructible robotic cop, using a dead police officer, a roll of aluminium foil and some old coins from the back of the sofa. A little-known fact: after the end credits on the first issue VHS cassette, the viewer is provided with full assembly instructions and can build his or her own fully weaponised robotic companion.

[30] *Killer astronaut from Mars*

I am seven years old. Today I am writing a story and my story is about my daddy's friend. He is called Warwick Lancaster. He worked for NASA which is the National Advanced Space Astronauts and he is very clever. I think most astronauts are clever and always pass exams. I don't like exams because you have to remember things but I am not good at remembering things. I like little baby monkeys in nappies. I have to call him Mister Lancaster the Astronaut Man but I don't want to. Warwick had an astronaut diary and he wrote what he did in it every day. When I found the astronaut diary I was amazed at what he wrote. Now you can read the astronaut diary.

Monday

Today I woke up and brushed my teeth. I like Crunchy Nut Corn Flakes. Then I went to work. I work at NASA. It is a very big building full of scientists. A scientist is a person who is so good at science and there are also people with normal jobs like accountants. I am an astronaut and sometimes I get to fly into space and other planets. It is really cool when it is time for launch which we also call blast off. I have a badge. Today we went into space for a little while to check it out. When I go into space I have to wear my space suit. If I don't then I won't be able to breathe properly and I might get poorly. My suit looks very excellent. People always tell me that when I go to fancy dress parties and I always have the best costume. When I was in space today I could see Earth from far. You can see all the water and mountains but no people because they are small when you are in space. I don't know if you can see trucks and vans but I didn't see any. Minis are too small but they look good in red. I could also see the Moon close up. It had some holes in it and it is hotter up in space because you are closer to the Sun. When you jump it is like you are flying because you go very high. Some of my friends are also astronauts but I am the best at being an astronaut because I can run fast. Today I got a NASA mission and we are going to the Moon to see what is going on up there because we went there a long time ago. We have mostly been going to see other planets now. We are going to fly out soon. I'm the leader of the astronauts and everyone has to call me Captain which I like sometimes but sometimes it is cooler to be called an astronaut and sometimes I wish they called me Captain Astronaut because that is what I am. They work hard even though they are not as good as me.

Tuesday

Today I started astronaut training. It was very hard work and then I was tired. First I spent some time doing weights. I managed to lift more than anyone else which is normal for me because I am strong and have big muscles. They are hard. Then I had a go on the giant spinny wheel and you have to stand inside it and it spins around a lot to make you dizzy. You have to try to make it stop being spinny if you can and the faster you can make it stop the better you are at it. I was the fastest at the spinny wheel and got to have 2 goes. I like going on it but it makes some people not feel well. Paul wasn't good at it and then he ran to the toilet and he never told me why but I saw a bit of porridge on his chin after.

Wednesday

Today was the mission. We got into the spaceship and counted down. 3... 2...1... BLAST OFF! It's fun when you get to shout BLAST OFF! but sometimes it scares my cat because it is loud. He is called Russell and he is soft like candy floss but I don't eat Russel. It's really cool when you start flying in space. It is dark up there but once we got into space we could take off our seat belts. Then I told the astronauts their jobs and then I started to drive to the moon. The journey was quite long and after a couple of hours I could not see any more trucks. But suddenly the spaceship moved about but not like I wanted it to. I looked out the window and there were big giant rocks and some did hit into the spaceship. But I am a great space pilot and I flew the spaceship around them and the rocks didn't hit the spaceship any more and then we were safe. But the alarm started going off and I looked at the screen and it said that there was something that it didn't know in the spaceship. So I went to see what it was and I looked around for a while and I found out it was an alien with a gun! It had green skin and big eyes and the big gun that it pointed at me and I wanted to stop it from hurting me so I jumped onto it and then we fell into one of the escape boxes which is like a little spaceship for when you need to escape and the door closed on us. We carried on fighting for a bit but it was a very strong alien and put me in a coma no problem.

Wednesday evening

When I woke up the alien was gone and the escape box was in space. I could not even see the spaceship or the Moon or anything. It was not a good time to wake up. I looked out of the window and I could see the stars but NASA made me look at pictures of stars all day long when I was learning to be an astronaut so when I looked outside I knew where I was. I was flying to Mars and a few hours later I landed on Mars. It was quite empty but after a little while some aliens came up to me and they looked like the one that I had a fight with but they had guns too. One of them did point a gun at my face and just then I wished it was dead. Suddenly it fell onto the floor and melted and the other aliens looked at the melted alien and then they put their weapons down and did bow to me. That was really wicked if you saw it. I was a bit confused and I think they did think that I made the alien die. Now I was like their master or something. They asked me what I wanted and I said water and they brought me water and then they asked me again and I said chocolate and they brought me chocolate and then they asked me again and I said a house and they made me a house but that took a bit longer. It was OK and it had a chimney and a garden and a swing and a slide.

Thursday

I woke up and my new house was brilliant. It had a TV and it had a computer and a trampoline and lots of sweets. The aliens made what I wanted. If any of them messed about I wished that they died and then they melted and there was green lumps. Soon I worked out that my brain was doing the murders. Then I told them that I wanted to be an actress and they made me into an actress. It was a good day.

Friday

Today I drove around really fast in my Pontiac Trans Am that the aliens made for me. The aliens are pretty cool but today I miss my friends and the other astronauts so I did ask the aliens for a spaceship so I can go back home. It will be ready tomorrow and I can't wait.

Saturday

Today my new spaceship was made for me. The aliens were making it all night. It was very nice and I got inside and then I started the engine and then it was all working fine so I shouted BLAST OFF! and then I was happy because I would be home soon.

Sunday

I think the aliens are stupid aliens because they did not put enough petrol in and I ran out of petrol. The spaceship is floating around and it is scary and I don't know what to do.

Monday

Today I almost wished I was dead and that is all because I am really sad. I have nearly run out of chocolate as well.

Tuesday

I have run out of chocolate. I wish I was

[31] The inventor of the classroom space-saving tray, Professor Raymond Buster-MacLean, went on to live a long and happy life and eventually passed away at the age of 103, peacefully in his tent. His other inventions include the carrier bag, suppositories, roofs, and carp.

[32] *Jazzy* is another word that was once used to describe them.

www.ingramcontent.com/pod-product-compliance
Ingram Content Group UK Ltd.
Pitfield, Milton Keynes, MK11 3LW, UK
UKHW040557210726
13854UKWH00008B/1376